D1442384

Dachshund

Charles and Linda George

Created by Q2AMedia
www.q2amedia.com
Editor Jeff O' Hare
Publishing Director Chester Fisher
Client Service Manager Santosh Vasudevan
Project Manager Kunal Mehrotra
Art Director Harleen Mehta
Designer Pragati Gupta
Picture Researcher Nivisha Sinha

Library of Congress Cataloging-in-Publication Data
Dachshund / [Charles George,Linda George].
p. cm. — (Top dogs)
Includes index.
ISBN 0-531-23243-3/978-0-531-23243-9 (hardcover)
1. Dachshunds—Juvenile literature. I. Title. II. Series.
SF429.D25D24 2010
636.753'8—dc22
2010035032

This edition published by Scholastic Inc.,

Printed and bound in Heshan, China
232657 10/10
10 9 8 7 6 5 4 3 2 1

Picture Credits
t= top, b= bottom, c= center, r= right, l= left

Cover Page: Liliya Kulianionak/Istockphoto.

Title Page: Hannamariah/Shutterstock.

4: Liotru/Shutterstock; 4-5: Simaha/Istockphoto; 5cl: Kuzma/Shutterstock;
5tr: Willee Cole/Shutterstock; 6-7: Liliya Kulianionak/Istockphoto; 8: Kim Ruoff/
Shutterstock; 8-9: Valpictures/Fotolia; 10: Erik Isakson/Photolibrary; 10-11: Children
Photos/Shutterstock; 12-13: Liliya Kulianionak/Shutterstock, Pablo H Caridad/Shutterstock;
14: Joe Lena/Istockphoto; 15: Kais Tolmats/Istockphoto; 16: Joe Lena/Istockphoto;
17: Kudrashkaa/Shutterstock; 18-19: Yan Wen/Shutterstock; 20-21: Jean Frooms/Istockphoto;
22-23: YinYang/Istockphoto; 23: Mark Herreid/Shutterstock; 24: Shinya Sasaki/Neovision/
Getty Images; 25: Mark Herreid/123RF; 26-27: Andrey Sukhanov 28-29: Jiri Hubatka/
Photolibrary; 30-31: www.dogimages.org.uk; 31: Aerial Focus.

Contents

What are Dachshunds?

Dachshunds (*daks-hoonts*) are from Germany. They were first used for hunting badgers. Badgers are small animals that live underground. Dachshund means "badger dog" in German.

Fast Fact

Some people call dachshunds "Weenie Dogs." They think these dogs are shaped liked wieners or hot dogs.

Denmark

Kiel

Rostock

Lübeck

Hamburg

Poland

Oldenburg

Bremen

Holland

Hannover

Wolfsburg

Berlin

Osnabrück

Potsdam

Münster

Bielefeld

Braunschweig

Magdeburg

Germany
Deutschland

Cottbus

Essen

Dortmund

Düsseldorf

Kassel

Leipzig

Köln

Siegen

Erfurt

Dresden

Belgium

Aachen

Bonn

Koblenz

Frankfurt am M.

Czech Rep.

Wiesbaden

Mannheim

Würzburg

Saarbrücken

Kaiserslautern

Nürnberg

Regensburg

France

Stuttgart

Ingolstadt

Reutlingen

Ulm

München

Freiburg

Austria

Switzerland

Dachshunds were good hunting dogs. In addition to badgers, they also hunted foxes and rabbits. Long-haired dachshunds were also used for hunting birds. Some dachshunds had hair that protected them while they were hunting.

Fast Fact

Some dachshunds have long hair. Some have short, smooth hair. Others have **wiry** hair.

5

Everyone Loves Dachshunds

Dachshunds come in different colors. Some are red and cream. Others are black and tan. Some are chocolate and tan. Still others can be gray and tan.

Fast Fact

Dachshunds were first brought to the U.S. in the late 1800s.

Fast Fact

Walking your dachshund helps it get used to other animals and people.

Dachshunds make good pets for small houses. They are fun-loving. They like spending time with their owners. Dachshunds are very friendly with people they know. They can be shy around strangers.

Dachshunds and Kids

Dachshunds like children. They love being part of whatever the family is doing. Be careful around a dachshund. They might **snap** at kids they don't know. They also might bite if they are teased or treated badly.

Fast Fact

Give a dachshund time to get to know you before you try to pet it.

Dachshunds like to run and play outside. They are **curious** about new things. They like to explore. They also like to dig! They are hunters. So, they like playing **fetch**. They like hunting for a thrown ball.

Fast Fact

Dachshunds need toys to chew. They pick them up and shake them!

A dachshund puppy weighs about 6 to 10 ounces (0.17-0.28 kg) when it is born. That's not very heavy! A dachshund puppy is about as big as a hot dog. It is almost the same shape, too!

Fast Fact

A puppy's eyes don't open until it is about ten days old. Before then, its eyes aren't ready to see.

Your puppy will **nurse** from its mother for about six weeks. Don't take your puppy away from its mother too soon. It may cry. Until your puppy is ready to leave its mother, play with it close to her. Then, your puppy won't get upset.

Teeny Weenies

Dachshund puppies are lovable and sweet. They lie next to their mother to stay warm. They are very small. Be sure to handle them with care. Be gentle with them.

Fast Fact

Most dachshund **litters** have four or five puppies.

A dachshund puppy loves to play. Then, it gets tired and sleeps. Even if you want to keep playing, let your puppy nap. It needs many naps to build up its energy!

Fast Fact

Dachshund puppies like to sleep curled up like a doughnut!

Taking Care of Your Dachshund

Does your dachshund puppy have toys to chew? Its teeth itch when they start growing in. This is called **teething**. Chewing on things helps make your dachshund's teeth feel better.

Fast Fact

Dachshund puppies need to meet other dogs and people, beginning when they are very young.

Be careful when you take your puppy outside to play. It is very small. It might get under your feet or between your legs. It could get stepped on when it runs. Lie on the grass to play with your puppy.

Fast Fact

If your puppy gets scared, hold it up close to your neck. Talk softly to it. It might try to suck on your ear!

Brushing Hair and Clipping Nails

Be careful when you brush your dachshund. Don't brush too hard. Always brush from head to tail. Your dachshund will love having its back scratched!

Fast Fact

Most dogs shed. Brushing removes some of the loose hair.

Are your dachshund's nails rough? If they are, they need to be trimmed. A pet doctor, or veterinarian, should do this. Your vet will check your dachshund's ears, too. If there are insects in its ears, the vet will remove them.

Fast Fact

Your dog's claws may naturally wear down on the pavement if you take it for a walk every day.

How Big do Dachshunds Get?

Mini dachshunds grow to be about 5-6 inches (12.7-15.2 cm) tall. Regular dachshunds are 8-9 inches (20.3-22.9 cm) tall. Mini dachshunds weigh up to 11 pounds (5.0 kg). Regular dachshunds weigh between 16 and 32 pounds (7.3-14.5 kg).

Fast Fact

Some people say that a dachshund is "two dogs long, but only half a dog high."

It is important to pick up your dachshund in the right way. If you don't, you could hurt its long back. The best way to hold a dachshund is the way a football player carries a football. Be sure your dog's back stays straight.

Fast Fact

Hundreds of years ago, dachshunds were larger than they are now.

Dashing Dachshunds

Dachshunds have short legs. But they love to run. They are hunting dogs. They enjoy sniffing for small animals like mice and rabbits. They also like to chase them. Dachshunds like to dig. They may dig holes in your garden!

Fast Fact

Hide one of your dog's toys. When it finds the toy, it'll be very happy!

Smooth or long-haired dachshunds may be quiet dogs. Wire-haired dachshunds may have more energy. Mini dachshunds are more timid than their bigger cousins. All these dogs love going for walks on a **leash**.

Fast Fact

A **harness** won't hurt your Dachshund's neck if it pulls too hard on the leash.

Make Room for Your Dachshund!

Does your dachshund live inside? Take it out every day to play or for a walk. It has short legs. Your dog won't have to walk very far to get enough exercise.

Fast Fact

Four blocks is probably far enough for most dachshunds to walk.

Take your dachshund to a park with trees, shrubs, or bushes. Your dachshund wants to sniff where other animals have been. It would love to hunt these animals. A dachshund doesn't get to hunt anymore, but it still likes doing it!

Fast Fact

Don't let your dachshund gain too much weight. Being overweight can hurt its back.

Smart Dogs

Dachshunds are not easy to **train**. They can be **stubborn**. Be patient. Dogs need to know how to behave. Dachshunds are curious. They get bored easily. Keep training sessions short.

Your dog may lose interest in being trained. If it does, play with your dachshund for a while. When it's tired, try another short training session. You may have to repeat the lessons many times.

Fast Fact

Sometimes, a dachshund can't do things that other dogs can do. But it will still try!

Earthdog Trials and Field Trials

A dachshund enjoys **Field Trials** and **Earthdog Tests**. A cage of small animals is placed in a burrow. A dog is let loose in the burrow. Judges see how long it takes the dog to reach the cage.

Fast Fact

Dachshunds will crawl into an animal's burrow. Their short legs make this pretty easy.

Dachshunds love to sniff out small animals. They follow the animal's scent back to its burrow. A burrow is a tunnel leading to an underground home. Dachshunds have a sharp sense of smell!

Fast Fact

In some trials, dachshunds track rabbits by following their scent.

Dachshunds Helping People

Dachshunds are good **companions**. They like snuggling with people. They like sleeping in a cozy bed. Sometimes, they like sleeping on the end of your bed.

Fast Fact

Don't be surprised if your dachshund tunnels under your covers on a cold night!

Dachshunds are friendly dogs. They love people. This makes them good **therapy dogs**. Therapy dogs visit sick people and people who live alone. They can help people get well. Petting dogs makes a person feel better.

Fast Fact

Dog petting isn't just good for people. It's good for the dog, too.

Best of the Breed

Some dachshunds are show dogs. Their owners train them to enter dog shows. The American Kennel Club (AKC) has **dog shows** every year. Many dogs compete to see who will win.

Fast Fact

Dog shows are sometimes shown on TV. It's fun to watch the dogs!

30

A mini dachshund named Brutus was named the "Highest **Skydiving** Dog." He wears **goggles** and rides in a pouch on his owner's chest. This keeps him safe when they jump out of the airplanes.

Fast Fact

Brutus loves jumping out of airplanes!

Glossary

Companion – friend

Curious – interested in exploring and discovering new things

Dog show – a contest between dogs to see which dog is the best in its breed

Earthdog Trial – a contest to see how fast a dog can follow a burrow to find animals in a cage

Fetch – a game played by throwing something for a dog to retrieve

Field Trial – a contest to see which dog can track a rabbit or other small animal the best

Goggles – special glasses worn to protect the eyes

Harness – a web of straps that fits around a dog's chest and neck

Leash – a strap that attaches to a collar or harness, to help control a dog on a walk

Litter – a group of puppies or other animals born to a mother, at the same time

Nurse – drink milk from a mother's breast

Retrieve – bring back

Scent – a smell or odor

Skydiving – jumping out of an airplane with a parachute

Snap – try to bite

Stubborn – unwilling to change

Teething – when new teeth grow in

Wiry, wire-haired – having coarse, stiff hair

Index